Seven Steps to Success
The Part 1 MRCOG Examination

*Includes 2 full specimen
examination papers,
Complete with EMQs & MCQs*

S. J. Duthie

Seven Steps to Success
The Part 1 MRCOG Examination

Mr S John Duthie

Dalton Square Medical Ltd

Also available…

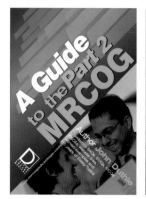 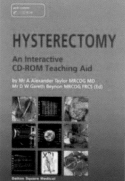 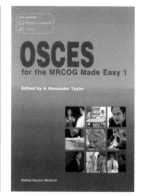

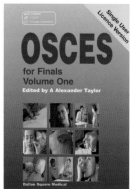 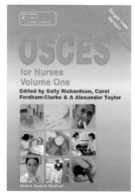 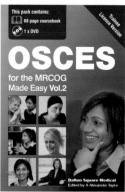

A Guide to the Part 2 MRCOG by S.J.Duthie
ISBN 978-0-9555690-3-6
Hysterectomy An Interactive CD-ROM Teaching Aid
ISBN 978-0-9541732-1-X
OSCES for the MRCOG Made Easy Volume 1 (trainee version)
ISBN 978-0-9541732-2-8
OSCES for Finals Volume 1 (single user version)
ISBN 978-0-9541732-7-9
OSCES for Nurses Volume 1 (single user version)
ISBN 978-0-9555690-0-5
OSCES for the MRCOG Made Easy Volume 2 (Home Edition)
ISBN 978-0-9555690-1-2

You can order titles, from your local bookshop or directly from Dalton Square Medical at
www.Daltonsquaremedical.co.uk

Seven Steps to Success
The Part 1 MRCOG Examination

Author

Mr S John Duthie MBBS MRCOG

Consultant Obstetrician & Gynaecologist
Blackpool Fylde and Wyre Hospitals NHS Foundation Trust

Published by Dalton Square Medical Ltd

© Dalton Square Medical Ltd 2009

Dalton Square Medical Ltd a company registered in England and Wales under number 6572579 and whose registered office is at PO Box 6587, Bournemouth, Dorset, BH4 OBL

Edited by A Alexander Taylor

First published 2009

ISBN 978-0-9555690-4-3

British Library Cataloguing in Publication Data
A catalogue record for this book is available from the British Library

Library of Congress Cataloguing in Publication Data
A catalogue record for this book is available from the Library of Congress

Note
Medical knowledge is constantly changing. As new information becomes available, changes in treatment, procedures, equipment and the use of drugs become necessary. The author, editor and publisher have, as far as it is possible, taken care to ensure that the information given in this text is accurate and up to date. However, readers are strongly advised to confirm that the information, especially with regard to drug usage, complies with the latest legislation and standards of practice.

Printed in England by Colin Cross Printers 01995 604368

Contents

Foreword

Membership of the Royal College of Obstetricians and Gynaecologists is essential for those wishing to practice Obstetrics and Gynaecology at Consultant level in the United Kingdom, and is a highly sought after qualification for many colleagues from other parts of the World. Discontinuation of the system of exemption from Part 1 MRCOG for those who pass local exams in the speciality has meant that possession of the Part 1 is the only route towards Part 2 and eventual Membership. The curriculum and syllabus for the Part 1 have been extensively revised over the past decade, in part to meet the requirements of the UK Postgraduate Medical Training and Education Board but also in recognition of the need to update the breadth of the science covered in the exam.

Candidates no longer need worry about the anatomy of the lymphatic duct or the cerebellum but can expect questions on relevant areas of molecular biology and genetics, biophysics and biostatistics. Up to date knowledge in these rapidly moving areas can make the difference between pass and fail.

Mr Duthie and his colleagues are to be congratulated on producing a comprehensive, readable and contemporary guide to the Part 1 MRCOG.

The book reflects the recent changes and updates to the Part 1 syllabus and it will be of great help to those preparing for the exam, and should become required reading at this level. The standard and style of the extended matching questions closely parallels that of the exam itself, and the inclusion of a mock Part 1 paper will allow candidates to work under exam conditions and self-assess. The book fills a large gap in the available literature and will be of use to all our candidates both in UK and elsewhere in the World.

Professor W. Ledger

Introduction

I have enjoyed writing this book for many reasons. I find our specialty fascinating. It is based on discovery, the creation of models to aid understanding and above all it is driven by a desire to help the women under our care. The Part 1 MRCOG Examination is an essential step in becoming a full member of the Royal College of Obstetricians and Gynaecologists. This book has been written with the needs and worries of the candidates foremost in my thoughts. The contents of the book include seven key topics. These are by no means the seven most important topics or the most difficult lessons to learn. They are simply seven issues that potential candidates must know about, often find confusing and about which candidates have to look in different places to gain sufficient knowledge. The "Seven Steps to Success" are followed by two full specimen papers which I hope will be representative of the actual examination in standard, style and use of different formats. Please allow yourself the appropriate time to attempt the specimen papers under undisturbed examination conditions. Some of the items are based on what is covered in the first section. All the answers are provided.

I hope that you enjoy reading the book as much as I have enjoyed writing it.

Suresh John Duthie FRCOG
Blackpool

About the author

John Duthie is a Consultant Obstetrician and Gynaecologist at the Blackpool, Fylde and Wyre Hospitals NHS Trust. He graduated in medicine at Liverpool University and took up a Lectureship in Obstetrics and Gynaecology at the University of Hong Kong, followed by posts as Senior Registrar in Liverpool and Chester. He was appointed a full-time consultant in 1995. For many years he has been passionate about medical education. He was appointed as an examiner for the DRCOG in 1997 and for the MRCOG in 2001. He served on the Part 2 EMQ committee as a founding member from its inception in 2003 to 2006. He has taught on several of the MRCOG revision courses and was co-convener of the official Royal College Part 2 Revision Course from 2005 to 2008. In March 2007 he was sponsored by the College to visit and liaise with the National Board of Medical Examiners in Philadelphia, USA on item development and assessment of test validity. This is his fourth textbook; previous texts, including two covering MRCOG EMQs have been bestsellers and well-reviewed and he has many publications in peer-reviewed journals. He is a founding member of the new RCOG Assessment Committee. John Duthie was appointed Convenor of the Royal College of Obstetricians and Gynaecologists' Training the Trainers courses in 2009.

Using the mrcogadvantage.com website and Dalton Square Medical Resources

This website would be of interest to candidates preparing for the Part 1 MRCOG examination. The site offers test papers with online marking. Do remember that it can take several hours to attempt the various papers under examination conditions. Practice makes perfect.

Once you've succeeded in passing Part 1, one of the best ways of preparing for the Part 2 is to buy my Guide to the Part 2 MRCOG, published by Dalton Square Medical Ltd. For OSCE preparation I would recommend you purchase, OSCEs for the MRCOG Made Easy Volume 1 & Volume 2. The latter has recently been "Highly Recommended" by the British Medical Association, in the 2009 BMA book competition. It provides gold standard, filmed OSCEs, with a particular focus on communication issues and tips on how to maximize your communication skills.

Good luck!

 # Step 1

The Ureter

A thorough knowledge of this organ in important for the Obstetrician and Gynaecologist. Its embryology, anatomy, surgical anatomy and pathology are fertile grounds for the development of Part 1 and Part 2 MRCOG examination items. The reader is well advised to read standard textbooks on the subject but here are a few helpful notes;

Embryology

The ureters develop from the ureteric buds of the mesonephric ducts. The mesonephric ducts form in the intermediate mesoderm of the embryo at around day 24. At this stage the mesonephric "ducts" are actually solid and are located in the thoraxic region of the embryo lying dorsolateral to the mesonephric tubules. Over the next 2 days the mesonephric "ducts" grow into the lower lumbar region, separate from the intermediate mesoderm and fuse with the cloaca on Day 26. An understanding of the fusion between the mesonephric ducts and the cloaca is important;

a) the site of fusion becomes part of the posterior wall of the bladder
b) the site of fusion is at the venterolateral part of the cloaca
c) at the time of fusion a process of canalisation commences and proceeds in a cranial direction, thus producing the mesonephric ducts.

The renal nephrons arise from the metanephric blastema. The nephron consists of Bowman's capsule, the proximal convoluted tubule, the loop of Henle with its descending and ascending limbs and the distal convoluted tubule. The ureteric buds differentiate into the ureters and collecting system of the kidneys. The metanephric blastema originates from the intermediate mesoderm in the sacral region. Therefore, the kidneys and ureters have a twofold origin and arise from the mesoderm. The blood supply of the kidneys comes from the aorta. As the kidneys advance from their original sacral site to a lumbar site between the sixth and ninth weeks the arterial supply comes from a series of transient branches from the paired dorsal aortae. As the developing kidneys advance the branches from the aortae disappear and are replaced by more cranial vessels with the renal arteries ultimately originating from the aorta. The renal arteries are, therefore, the final pair of arteries in the succession of arteries to the developing kidneys. If an earlier pair of arteries persist, the renal arteries will be at an inferior level to the renal arteries and are referred to as accessory renal arteries.

On day 32 the ureteric buds start to penetrate the metanephric blastema. This leads to a complex interaction of inductive signals from the metanephric blastema to the ureteric bud and vice versa. Biochemical signals from the ureteric bud are thought to guide the differentiation of tissue in the metanephric blastema into nephrons (Bowman's capsule and renal tubules). Reciprocal signals from the metanephric blastema induce the sequential differentiation of the ureteric bud. The signals are necessary for normal development. If the signals are missing or abnormal the correct structures will not form. Without a normal ureteric bud, the metanephric blastema will not develop into a kidney.

The ureteric bud forms the ipsilateral collecting tubules, minor calyces, major calyces, the renal pelvis and the ureter. The tips of the distal convoluted tubules become connected to the collecting ducts during the tenth week. At this stage, urine which is formed in the nephron can pass into the collecting duct, through the minor and major calyces, the renal pelvis and into the ureter.

Consider this extended matching question (EMQ);

List of options

A. Accessory renal artery
B. Bifid ureter
C. Horseshoe kidney
D. Pelvic kidney
E. Renal agenesis
F. Renal artery stenosis
G. Renal dysplasia
H. Simple renal cyst
I. Ureteric diverticulum
J. Ureteric duplication

The list of options contains different abnormalities of the urinary tract. The items below refer to embryonic events in the human embryo. For each scenario described in the items below, select the single most likely outcome from the list of options. Each option may be used once, more than once or not at all.

1. On day 28 the ureteric bud underwent bifurcation. The upper branch ended in a blind loop and the lower branch then penetrated the metanephric blastema. The lower end was undivided and attached normally to the bladder with ongoing development.

   Answer – B

2. The mesonephric duct gave rise to 2 ureteric buds on the same side. On day 32 both ureteric buds penetrated the metanephric blastema independently. The ureteric buds induced formation of renal nephrons. Both the tracts emptied urine into the bladder.

   Answer - J

3. The mesonephric duct failed to give rise to a ureteric bud on one side. Therefore, inductive signals did not arrive in the ipsilateral metanephric blastema.

   Answer –E

4. The inferior poles of the 2 developing kidneys fused together forming a continuous organ. There were 2 ureters. Ascent of the organ was arrested as the kidney was caught under the inferior mesenteric artery.

   Answer – C

The purpose of the EMQ is to test the examinee's understanding of applied embryology.

Anatomy

The anatomy of the ureter is fundamental to pelvic surgery. It is something that just has to be remembered; also useful for the Part 1 MRCOG examination! Here are some notes which you may find helpful;

1. The ureter in the adult female is between 25cm and 30cm in length. The organ drains the kidney of urine and connects the renal sinus with the urinary bladder.

2. The ureter has 3 coats or layers; fibrous, muscular, mucous.

3. The ureter passes downwards and medially in front of the psoas major muscle and passes into the pelvis.

4. The pelvic portion of the ureter passes downwards on the lateral pelvic wall along the anterior border of the greater sciatic notch. The ureter is under the cover of the peritoneum and forms the posterior boundary of the ovarian fossa.

5. As the ureter runs medially and forwards under the broad ligament and opposite the lower part of the greater sciatic foramen, it passes above the lateral fornix of the vagina.

6. It is important to note that the ureter lies anterior to the internal iliac artery and medial to the following structures; the obturator nerve and the umbilical, obturator, inferior vesical and middle rectal arteries. The uterine artery arises from the anterior division of the internal iliac artery, runs medially along the Levator ani muscle and crosses above and in front of the ureter at a point 2 cm lateral to the cervix.

7. The ureter finally enters the bladder obliquely.

8. The blood supply to the ureter reflects its path as it is supplied by branches from the following arteries; renal, gonadal, internal iliac, common iliac and inferior vesical.

An Obstetrician and Gynaecologist who understands the embryology and anatomy of the ureter would recognise its position in surgery, realise that there may be a duplicate or bifid ureter and have an understanding of how the organ may be damaged or involved in pathological processes.

Step 2

The Mast cell

Definitely worth knowing. The mast cell is located immediately outside most capillaries. It is similar to the circulating basophil. Mast cells and basophils contain histamine and they are the chief sites of storage of that substance. The mast cell contains the enzyme L-histidine decarboxylase. This enzyme catalyses the decarboxylation of the amino acid histidine to form histamine. Secretory granules within mast cells contain histamine, heparin and proteases.

It is important to note that histamine is also formed and stored in cells other than mast cells and basophils. These include neurons, regenerating tissues and the gastric mucosa. The amount of histamine in cerebrospinal fluid is significant.

The mast cells release the following substances;
Histamine
Heparin
Bradykinin
Serotonin
Eosinophil chemotactic factor

Immunoglobulin E has a special predisposition to attach to mast cells and basophils. A single mast cell can bind up to 500,000 molecules of IgE. If a specific antigen reacts with the IgE the mast cell (or basophil in the circulation) ruptures and releases significant quantities of the substances which are produced in those cells. The resulting vascular and tissue responses manifest as an allergic reaction. The activated mast cell also plays a key role in inflammation and in combating infection.

Consider the following EMQ;

A. Basophil
B. Colony forming unit-spleen
C. Eosinophil
D. Erythrocyte
E. Kupffer cell
F. Mast cell
G. Megakaryocyte
H. Neutrophil
I. Reticulocyte
J. Platelet

Select the single most correct type of cell from the list of options for the descriptions in each of the items below. Each item may be used once, more than once or not at all.

1. The cell contained a nucleus, there were granules in the cytoplasm and it was located outside a capillary. There were several hundred thousand IgE molecules attached to the cell membrane. In response to specific stimuli the cell secreted substances into the surrounding tissue leading to vasodilatation, increased capillary permeability and contraction of local smooth muscle.

    Answer –F

2. The cell contained a nucleus and it was located immediately outside a capillary. The cell contained the enzyme L-histidine decarboxylase which catalysed a key step in the synthesis of a molecule which contained an imidazole ring. The cell also synthesised heparin. These substances were stored in secretory granules with a pH of 5.5

    Answer –F

The description in both items is clearly that of the mast cell. What is the significance of the pH of the secretory granule? At this pH histamine is positively charged and forms an ionic complex with negatively charged acidic groups in other molecules such as heparin.

Step 3

Medical Physics

Electromagnetic Radiation

Obstetrics and Gynaecology depends, in part, on advanced technologies. There are several important reference books which the reader may consult. The important lesson in this text is one concerning electromagnetic radiation.

What is electromagnetic radiation? Electromagnetic radiation is the emission of energy as electromagnetic waves from a source. The energy in an electromagnetic wave is carried by oscillating electric and magnetic forces. What is important to note is that the electric and magnetic forces are at right angles to the direction in which the wave travels. The full electromagnetic spectrum consists of the following;

Approximate Wavelength

Cosmic radiation	10^{-6} nm
Gamma radiation	10^{-3} nm
X-rays	1nm- 0.001nm
Ultraviolet radiation	1nm-100nm
Visible light	380nm-750nm
Infrared radiation	750nm-1mm
Microwaves	1mm-10cm
Television broadcasts	10cm-10m
Radio waves	greater than 10m

Anyone studying basic science as applied to Obstetrics and Gynaecology would be well advised to learn something of the seven types of electromagnetic radiation ranging from cosmic rays to microwaves. Why? Many reasons, here are some of them.

The part of the spectrum from cosmic rays to ultraviolet rays, is considered to have the potential to damage DNA and produce mutations. The part of the spectrum from cosmic rays to X-rays is ionising. If ionising radiation strikes an atom or a molecule with a neutral charge and displaces an electron (or electrons) then a charged particle called an ion is formed. The ions and free radicals that result from the passage of electromagnetic radiation through a medium can themselves damage DNA. Let us look carefully at the first sentence in this paragraph. Ultraviolet rays have the potential to cause mutations if the exposure is excessive. Are ultraviolet rays ionising? No, they are not. This may be a useful way of understanding and remembering these fascinating facts. Cosmic rays, gamma rays and X-rays are ionising and mutagenic. Ultraviolet radiation is non-ionising but still mutagenic.

How does electromagnetic radiation cause damage to living cells? There are many different mechanisms; breaks in DNA, chromosomal deletions, translocations and aneuploidy, damage to proteins. Damage to cells by radiation is cumulative. This is of great clinical relevance when requesting imaging services. The radiation which is released affects the patient and contributes to background radiation.

Cosmic radiation

This is the term given to all the radiation from the sun and from the galaxies. There are two components; the solar component and the galactic component. Cosmic rays consist of a complex mixture of different radiations; some with very short wavelengths and some which are charged particles. Interesting...,but what has this got to do with Obstetrics and Gynaecology? Read on.

As stated previously, cosmic rays can lead to cell damage, mutations and are capable of causing illness. Who might be exposed to cosmic radiation? The Earth's magnetic fields deflect cosmic rays but do so unevenly. Human beings travelling in an aircraft at high altitude (which does include commercial jet flights) are exposed to cosmic rays more than those at ground level. Owing to the uneven deflection of cosmic rays, the exposure is higher at temperate latitudes towards the Earth's magnetic poles than near the equator. Also, exposure is higher at higher altitudes.

The Department of Transport in the United Kingdom has provided directives to airline operators regarding the protection of air crew from cosmic radiation. Applied to a pregnant woman who is a member of an air crew it is clearly stated that, once pregnancy is declared, the protection of the baby should be comparable with that provided for members of the public. In practice, many airline operators would "ground" a pregnant member of air crew. It is important to note that the risk of cosmic radiation is one of several conditions to consider. Pregnant women who work as air crew are also subject to risks associated with manual handling and exertion, dehydration, jet lag, injury and turbulence.

What are the quantifiable risks of exposure to cosmic radiation and how do they compare with the background risk? In the United Kingdom, the average dose of background radiation is 2.2 mSv (millisieverts) per annum. For a person flying on an aircraft at 10,000metres above sea level; on a 12 hour flight between London and Tokyo the estimated radiation dose is 58 microsieverts (0.058 millisieverts) and on a 7.5 hour flight between Sydney and Singapore the estimated radiation dose is 17 microsieverts. This difference in the radiation dose per hour of flying illustrates the fact that exposure is higher at temperate latitudes.

Monitoring of exposure is carried out using computer models. If the assessed annual dose is less than 6mSv per annum then the Directive from the Department of Transport does not require further action. The exposure of the human body to cosmic radiation (in an aircraft flying at altitude) is essentially uniform. The maternal abdomen does not shield the fetus. Therefore, it is to be considered that the equivalent dose to the fetus is equal to the dose of radiation received by the mother.

Gamma radiation

Gamma radiation is an electromagnetic radiation which is both ionising and mutagenic. Gamma rays are produced by the decay of radioactive nuclei such as those of Cobalt 60. There are many other sources of gamma rays, the point being that they have an intra-nuclear source. Gamma rays carry a lot of energy away from an emitting nucleus and then leave the nucleus in a more stable state. A short digression; what are alpha and beta rays? Alpha radiation is composed of helium nuclei; 2 protons and 2 neutrons (nucleon number 4, charge +2). They are released from certain radioactive nuclei. For example Uranium 238 releases an alpha particle to decay into Thorium 234. Alpha rays travel at a speed of 10^7 metres per second, have very strong ionising power but very poor penetration. Beta radiation is basically a stream of negatively charged electrons. Such a stream of electrons produced within and then emitted by a decaying radioactive nucleus is called a beta ray. Beta rays travel at a speed slightly below 3×10^8 metres per second, have medium ionising power and penetrate more than alpha particles but less than gamma rays. As beta rays are composed of relatively light electrons they can be deflected easily by a magnetic field. Alpha and beta radiation do NOT form part of the electromagnetic spectrum. Gamma rays travel at a speed of 3×10^8 metres per second, have weak ionising power and great penetration. Thus, gamma radiation is suitable for providing teletherapy.

Cobalt 60 (atomic number 27, nucleon number 60) emits gamma rays and is used as a source in various laboratories and has industrial, medical and commercial applications. The medical applications for gamma radiation include;

1. **Teletherapy of malignant disease**
2. **Sterilisation of instruments**
3. **Irradiation of blood**

The gamma radiation from Cobalt 60 has energy of 1.2 MeV (megavolts) but the beam has a comparatively high penumbra. This means that there is more of a shadow (penumbra) around the main beam. Please cross refer to the following section on X-rays.

What is "Cobalt 60"? An examination of the periodic table shows that the element cobalt, next to iron, has an atomic number of 27 and a nucleon number of 59 (atomic mass number). Is this the source of penetrating gamma radiation which can damage tissue deep within the body? No. It is the isotope cobalt 60 which is the source of gamma rays. Cobalt 60 is produced by the neutron activation of naturally occurring cobalt. The nucleus of cobalt 60 is unstable and decays by conversion of a neutron to a proton which remains in the nucleus and an electron which enters the electron shell. Its atomic mass number (number of protons and neutrons) is still 60 but the atomic number (number of protons) rises to 28 and the result is a nucleus of nickel. The activated nickel nucleus emits 2 gamma rays with energies of 1.17 and 1.33 MeV. The half life of cobalt 60 is 5.3 years.

X- rays

This is a type of electromagnetic radiation which has several medical applications.
The diagnostic X-ray has an energy of around 50 Kv (kilo volts). Therapeutic X-rays have energy levels approximately 600 times greater at around 30 MeV (mega volts). To produce megavoltage X-rays a linear accelerator is used to direct electrons at high speed onto a target. The target may be a substance such as gold or tungsten. The electrons strike the atoms and X radiation is released. This is the basis for megavoltage radiotherapy. If the target is removed the linear accelerator produces a high speed electron beam. This beam can be deflected and focused by magnetic fields for the same reasons that beta radiation from a nucleus can be manipulated. The electron beam has energy in excess of 30 MeV. This is the basis for electron beam teletherapy.
Compared with the gamma radiation from cobalt 60, megavoltage X-rays and electron beams offer some advantages. Megavoltage X-rays have a more precise beam with a narrower penumbra, there is less scattered radiation and a much higher dose of radiation can be delivered at greater depth. This means shorter treatment times.

In radiotherapy of malignant tumours, it is necessary to deliver an appropriate dose of radiation to the lesion while minimising the dose to normal tissues. A high dose of radiation may destroy the tumour but could also be lethal. Fractionation allows a higher total dose of radiation to be delivered. This entails the delivery of repeated course of radiation in modest doses thereby delivering a higher total dose than would be possible with a single and very high dose.

Consider the following MCQs to explore the previous section;

Cosmic radiation;

A. Consists in part of electromagnetic radiation with a
    wavelength less than 1 nanometer   **True**

B. Has an effective dose rate which increases with altitude
                                                        True

C. Exposure is higher near the equator than at temperate
    latitudes   **False**

D. Exposure should be less than 6 microsieverts per annum
                                                       False

E. Exposure to a pregnant woman results in equivalent
    doses to the woman and the baby in utero.   **True**

Cobalt 60;

A. Has an atomic number of 27   **True**

B. Has 33 neutrons in its nucleus   **True**

C. Emits beta radiation   **True**

D. Emits megavoltage X-rays   **False**

E. Occurs naturally   **False**

Rads, Grays and Sieverts

These are some of the units which are used to measure radiation and may become the source of much confusion.
1 Gray = 100 Rads. Therefore, one rad is sometimes called a centegray. The SI unit is Joule per kilogramme and shows the amount of energy absorbed by the target tissue. A Sievert is the equivalent dose to the target tissue. The nomenclature used by the International System of Units Measurements (SI units) is Joule per kilogramme.
Wait, that means that the Gray and the Sievert are both expressed as Joule per kilogramme!
Yes, but although the nomenclature is the same, the quantities that are being measured are quite different.
The Gray measures the radiation energy absorbed by the target tissue.
The Sievert measures the equivalent dose (of the absorbed dose) and is affected by the radiation weighting factor of a given radiation and the relative biological effectiveness. The radiation weighting factor is affected by the linear energy transfer of the radiation. One Gray of alpha radiation has a much greater effect than one Gray of neutron radiation which has a greater effect than one Gray of beta radiation. The ratio is considered to be 20 for alpha radiation, 10 for neutron radiation and 1 for beta radiation. The Sievert is also affected by the type of tissue which is being irradiated. The gonads with their rapidly dividing cells are highly radiosensitive and the surface of bone and the skin are not as radiosensitive. After the gonads, the bone marrow and colon are the most radiosensitive.

If the whole body receives an equivalent dose of 1 Sievert the effect is nausea. A higher dose of 2-5 Sieverts causes loss of hair, diarrhoea and bleeding. A dose of 6 Sieverts is uniformly lethal.

The Gray can be measured directly on target tissue. The Sievert is derived from the absorbed dose, the type of radiation and the nature of the irradiated tissue, its volume and the time over which the dose was given.

What is a nanometer?

A nanometer is a billionth of a meter or 1×10^{-9} m. This is the same as 10 Angstrom units. The non particulate components of cosmic rays have a wavelength of a millionth of a nanometer. Ultraviolet rays have wavelengths between 1 and 100 nm.
An idea of the size of the nanometer is useful as the sciences of nanotechnology and nanomedicine are rapidly developing.

Ultrasound

The application of diagnostic ultrasound has led to fundamental changes in Obstetric and Gynaecological practice. Ultrasound is the use of sound waves with certain qualities to provide imaging. By definition ultrasound has a frequency above that of the human audible range. Medical imaging uses ultrasound frequencies between 3 MHz and 10 MHz (mega Hertz). At a frequency of 3 MHz ultrasound waves have a wavelength of 0.5mm. At frequencies greater than 3 MHz the wavelength of ultrasound is even lower and the resolution is greater. However, attenuation of ultrasound by tissues is proportional to frequency. Attenuation is the reduction in the amplitude of a signal. Therefore, an ultrasound beam with a high frequency will be attenuated more than a beam with a lower frequency. Image quality is better with a higher frequency but the penetration of soft tissues is poor. What does this mean in practical terms? In pelvic scanning, an abdominal transducer would emit a beam with a frequency between 3.5 MHz and 5.0MHz and analyse the reflected echoes. A vaginal probe would employ a beam with a frequency of 7 MHz. Therefore, the quality of the image is better with a high frequency vaginal probe. On the other hand, soft tissue penetration is better with an abdominal probe using a lower frequency.

The transducer emits ultrasound and receives the reflected echoes. As a result of attenuation, the echoes from deeper interfaces will produce weaker signals than those nearer the transducer. The equipment has the ability to amplify signals from deeper interfaces and thereby compensate for the loss of energy. This is known as time gain compensation (TGC).

The equipment is also able to smooth or connect the dots in a digitised image. This is known as interpolation. Basically, the equipment analyses the known values of the digitised image, calculates the intervening points and then inserts them to produce an image.

How about Doppler physics? Consider the source of a wave and that which observes or reflects it. As the wave travels it has certain properties which include wavelength, amplitude and frequency. What happens if the source and reflector move? A moving source produces a Doppler shift in wavelength and a moving reflector produces a Doppler shift in frequency. The red shift noticed by astronomers is a Doppler effect. Distant galaxies emit light and move away from the Earth producing a shift in the wavelength of light towards the longer wavelengths; red light. Flowing erythrocytes clump irregularly in the blood vessels and these clumps act as reflectors of pulsed Doppler ultrasound. A Doppler shift in frequency occurs as the reflectors (groups of erythrocytes) move towards and away from the source. The equipment is able to analyse and display the difference between the sent and returning frequencies.

Remember that ultrasound is a form of sound. It is not a form of ionising radiation. However, tissue effects in terms of heating, cavitation and streaming of fluid are potential problems. The propagation speed of ultrasound waves in human soft tissue is 1,540 m/s. As they are sound waves, the propagation speed in solid tissue is higher. The propagation speed of ultrasound in bone is around 3,000 m/s.

The intensity of an ultrasound beam is expressed in terms of a quantity called "spatial peak temporal average intensity" or I_{spta}. This measure reflects the fact that ultrasound is a wave travelling within a space and its peak intensity is averaged over a specific time. What does all this mean for the Part 1 MRCOG candidate? (apart from the interesting physics!). Patient Safety. Different types of ultrasound have different I_{spta} values, allowing the operator the facility to reduce the ultrasound exposure to the minimum that is necessary. For instance the I_{spta} (measured in Watts/cm^2) is the least for B mode ultrasound, higher for M mode ultrasound, higher still for colour Doppler and maximal for pulsed Doppler spectrometry.

Consider this MCQ;

In obstetric ultrasound;

A. The frequency used by an abdominal transducer is 16 MHz **False**

B. A frequency of 7 MHz is suitable for a vaginal transducer **True**

C. The higher the frequency the lower the attenuation by soft tissues **False**

D. Time gain compensation partly corrects for attenuation **True**

E. The Doppler shift is due to a shift in frequency **True**

 **Step 4**

The Coefficient of Variability

The coefficient of variability is the standard deviation of a set of measurements with a normal distribution divided by the mean. Another way to express the coefficient of variability is μ/δ. Why is this important for a Part 1 MCOG candidate?

For several reasons;

it is useful to consider the coefficient of variability in assessments of reproducibility. Clinical governance demands that evidence based medicine is practised and that systems are in place to monitor exactly what is happening. Clearly, there is more to governance than that, but it is a source of useful examples to illustrate the point. Modern medicine demands accurate measurements.

In Obstetric ultrasound for example, a series of biometric measurements of the baby are taken. Who is carrying out the measurements?

How reliable and reproducible are the measurements?

Are there significant differences in measurement between different observers?

Are there significant differences within the same observer when he/she is asked to take repeat measurements of the same parameter on the same occasion?

Consider the following EMQ;

A. 0.01
B. 0.025
C. 0.05
D. 0.25
E. 0.5
F. 1
G. 1.25
H. 1.5

A large Obstetric service organised "dating" scans for pregnant women. It was envisaged that fetal gestational age would be determined by ultrasound examination of the pregnancy between 11 and 14 weeks. In order to assess quality control, the leads for the service selected pregnant women with a singleton pregnancy at a gestation of 11 completed weeks. The crown-rump length of the fetus in each woman was reliably measured as 5cm. For each item below, select the single most correct answer from the list of options. Each option may be used once, more than once or not at all.

1. One hundred different doctors, midwives and sonographers were asked to measure a crown-rump length of 5cm. The measurements were normally distributed around a mean of 5cm and the standard deviation was 0.25cm.Select the single most correct inter observer coefficient of variability from the list of options.

    Answer –C

2. Each scanner was asked to take 100 measurements of a crown-rump length of 5cm. For one individual the measurements were normally distributed around a mean of 5cm and the standard deviation was 0.25cm.Select the single most correct intra observer coefficient of variability from the list of options.

    Answer –C

In these 2 examples, the coefficient of variability was sufficiently small to have been considered as "acceptable". However, a large inter observer coefficient of variability indicates that some measurements are beyond what one would consider as acceptable.

This may reflect a need for training all staff to the same standard. A narrow intra observer coefficient of variability means that the measurements are reproducible and therefore reliable. A large intra observer coefficient of variability quite possibly reflects guesswork on the part of the observer rather than adherence to a standard.

Thus, the understanding of the coefficient of variability is an important step on the way to Part 1 MRCOG success.

Step 5

Folic Acid

A knowledge and understanding of this important water soluble vitamin is fundamental. Why? Folic acid is required for the synthesis of DNA by enabling the availability of purines and dTMP. Deficiency of folic acid is; one cause of megaloblastic anaemia, associated with an increased risk of neural tube defects in the offspring, associated with an increased risk of cancer of the colon and hyperhomocysteinaemia.

The concentration of folic acid in fetal serum is several times greater than that in maternal serum.

What is folic acid? It is pteroylmonoglutamic acid and occurs naturally as its polyglutamate derivatives. These "folic acid" substances are found in liver, green vegetables, limes and lemons and are soluble in water. When ingested, they enter the digestive system and are absorbed through the mucosa of the small intestine. The intestinal mucosa cells contain the enzyme glutamate conjugase which catalyses the conversion of polyglutamate residues to free folic acid. The next step involves the reduction of folic acid to tetrahydrofolic acid by the enzyme dihydrofolate reductase.
Circulating "folic acid" is actually a derivative of tetrahydrofolic acid.

What next? Soon, the relevance of all this will become clear. Tetrahydrofolic acid and Vitamin B_{12} are needed for the conversion of homocysteine to methionine. The substance methionine is required for protein synthesis. Also, it is converted to S-adenosylmethionine which is needed for the methylation of DNA. Inadequate tetrahydrofolic acid means inadequate conversion of homocysteine to methionine and hyperhomocysteinaemia results. Inadequate tetrahydrofolic acid leads to inhibition of DNA synthesis and an arrest of cells in S phase. These changes can have extensive clinical effects.

Is summary, so far, folic acid is found in liver, green vegetables, some fruits, is water soluble, absorbed through the small intestine, is reduced to tetrahydrofolic acid which is then used to convert homocysteine to methionine and the latter has critical roles in the synthesis of protein and DNA. Deficiency of folic acid may result from an inadequate intake, malabsorption, faulty metabolism and increased requirement.

3 other things to remember;

1. Folic acid is easily destroyed by heat.

2. Folic acid and Vitamin B_{12} are both required for the synthesis of DNA but they are involved in different reactions and are not interchangeable.

3. There is an increased requirement for folic acid during pregnancy and lactation.

The minimum daily requirement for folic acid during pregnancy is estimated to be 0.4mg or 400µg. In the United Kingdom this dose of folic acid is available "over the counter" whereas the dose of 5mg once daily per oram has to be prescribed. There are specific indications for using the higher dosage and these centre around the risk of having a child with a neural tube defect; a woman who has a previously affected child with open neural tube defect, a woman with diabetes mellitus and a woman who is taking anticonvulsants.

There is another interesting feature of enzyme biochemistry regarding folic acid metabolism. The enzyme MTHFR (5, 10 methylenetetrahydrofolate reductase) is necessary for one of the steps in the production of 5 methylenetetrahydrofolate from folic acid. If this enzyme MTFHR is deficient or abnormal then there is insufficient tetrahydrofolate for the conversion of homocysteine to methionine. Then, the serum homocysteine level rises. One clinical manifestation of deficiency in MTFHR in a woman in early pregnancy is a significantly increased risk of open neural tube defect.

Let us look a little more deeply into this lesson. A significant minority of Caucasians and Asians have a genetic polymorphism that affects the gene that codes for MTFHR. In their DNA there is a thymine for cytosine substitution and the result is that there is a substitution of the amino acid valine for the amino acid alanine in the polypeptide coded by the gene. The specific activity and stability of MTFHR are both affected. Approximately 12% of Caucasians and Asians are homozygous (thymine/thymine) for this genetic polymorphism. These individuals tend to have low serum folate levels and high serum homocysteine levels. In the presence of a low dietary intake of folic acid, the risk of open neural tube defect, in a woman who is homozygous for the genetic polymorphism that affects MTFHR is significantly raised.

The risk of cancer of the colon appears to be elevated in older people who are homozygous and who have a deficient folic acid intake.

The genetic polymorphism that affects the gene that codes for MTFHR influences the individual's response to folic acid deficiency. It must be stated however, that the causes of open neural tube defects in humans have not been fully elucidated. There are other factors aside from folic acid deficiency such as teratogens, exposure to a high tissue level of glucose and insulin.

Consider this EMQ;

A. Ascorbic acid
B. Cholecalciferol
C. Cyanocobalamin
D. Folic acid
E. Pyridoxine
F. Riboflavin
G. Thymine

Select the vitamin which is the single most likely to be deficient in the scenarios described in the items below. Each option may be used once, more than once or not at all.

1. A 24 year old woman had a homozygous genetic polymorphism that affected the gene that coded for the protein 5, 10 methylenetetrahydrofolate reductase (MTFHR). The woman had a diet that lacked fruit and vegetables and she disliked liver. As a result her serum homocysteine level was raised.

    Answer –D

2. A 24 year old woman had a homozygous genetic polymorphism that affected the gene that coded for the protein 5, 10 methylenetetrahydrofolate reductase (MTFHR). The woman had a diet that consisted for the large part on cereals, milk, and cranberry juice with very little meat. The woman had reduced her consumption of meat for the previous 6 months. Any vegetables which the woman ate were boiled thoroughly. The woman became pregnant. The caudal neuropore of the embryo did not close on day 26.

    Answer –D

3. A young woman developed a targeted gene mutation that affected coding of the enzyme glutamate conjugase in the cells of the intestinal mucosa. The activity of the enzyme was reduced. As a result the woman developed a severe megaloblastic anaemia.

    Answer -D

4. A young woman developed a defect in the parietal cells of her gastric mucosa and intrinsic factor production became deficient. As a result the woman developed a macrocytic anaemia.

    Answer -C

Consider these 2 MCQs;

Folic acid;

A.	Is absorbed in the small intestine	True
B.	Is soluble in water	True
C.	Is converted to methionine	False
D.	Is required for the synthesis of DNA	True
E.	Is necessary for the final maturation of red blood cells	True

Deficiency of folic acid is associated with;

A.	Elevated serum homocysteine	True
B.	Chronic alcoholism	True
C.	Use of methotrexate	True
D.	Haemolytic anaemia	True
E.	Anticonvulsant drugs	True

 **Step 6**

How Do I Calculate Creatinine Clearance?

First of all, why must I calculate 24 hour creatinine clearance? Clearance is the volume of plasma that contains the mass of a solute that is excreted by the kidneys per unit time. The units are ml/min. In other words; volume of plasma containing the amount of creatinine which is filtered is expressed as ml and time is expressed in minutes.

Creatinine is a product of muscle metabolism and is predominantly excreted by the kidneys by glomerular filtration. A small amount of creatinine is secreted by the renal tubules. Measurement of inulin clearance is a method of estimating the glomerular filtration rate as inulin is freely filtered by the glomerulus and is neither reabsorbed nor secreted. However, inulin is not produced in the human body and must be given as an intravenous injection. Therefore; measuring creatinine clearance is a useful means of estimating the glomerular filtration rate. Normal creatinine clearance in the non pregnant adult is about 120ml/min. During a normal pregnancy the creatinine clearance increases to 170ml/min and the serum urea and creatinine decrease. It is important to note that creatinine clearance must fall quite significantly before there are changes in serum urea and electrolytes. In women with renal failure the creatinine clearance falls. In the presence of severe gestational proteinuric hypertension, the creatinine clearance could fall significantly.

The creatinine clearance may be calculated from knowledge of serum creatinine, the concentration of creatinine in the urine and the volume of urine passed in 24 hours. The 24 hour urine sample enables an estimate of the typical volume of urine produced in one minute. Consider this example; a woman passes 1.5 litres of urine in 24 hours and the urinary concentration of creatinine is 5mmol/l. Her serum creatinine is 40µmol/l.

Therefore, the mass of creatinine that was passed over 24 hours was 7.5mmol. It is worth making an obvious but important point here. The concentration of creatinine in urine is much higher than in serum. In urine, the concentration of creatinine is expressed in millimoles per litre whereas in serum its concentration is expressed in micromoles per litre. Also, it is useful to remember that there are 1,440 minutes in 24 hours. It is implicit that 5.2 µmol of creatinine (7500/ 1440) are excreted by the kidneys in one minute. What volume of plasma would contain 5.2 µmol of creatinine?

Well, we know that 1,000 ml contains 40 µmol. Hence, 130 ml plasma (5200/40) would contain 5.2 µmol of creatinine. The creatinine clearance is 130ml/min.

Consider this MCQ;

Creatinine;

A. Contains a phosphate group   **False**

B. Is produced in skeletal muscle   **True**

C. Has a higher concentration in the renal vein than the renal artery   **False**

D. Is secreted by the renal tubules   **True**

E. Concentration falls sharply in a woman with acute renal failure   **False**

Creatinine is produced in muscle by the non-enzymatic conversion of creatine phosphate. It is then released into the circulation, reaches the kidneys via the renal arteries and excreted by the kidneys. The concentration in the renal vein is obviously lower than that in the renal artery.

Consider this EMQ;

A. μmol
B. μmol/min
C. μmol/ ml
D. mg
E. mg/min
F. mg/ml
G. ml
H. ml/min

Creatinine clearance is measured in different clinical settings as one method of assessment of renal function. Select the single most correct units for expressing creatinine clearance from the list of options.

Answer - H

# Step 7

Rubella

Rubella is a single stranded RNA virus with only one serotype. The organism causes a multi-system infection with minimal impact on adults but can be devastating to the fetus in utero. No antiviral chemotherapy is available at present but there is a vaccine which contains live attenuated virus. The effects of rubella on the fetus are maximal if infection occurs during the first trimester. Rubella produces a congenital infection which can be remembered as a triad; heart disease, cataracts and nerve deafness. There are several other malformations and illnesses caused by congenital rubella.

The 2 most common viral infections to infect the central nervous are rubella and cytomegalovirus (CMV). Following infection of the brain in the embryo both viruses cause necrotising encephalitis. The organ of Corti in the inner ear tends to be affected in cases of rubella and this is one reason for nerve deafness in affected children.

How does the rubella virus reach the fetus in utero? The virus is spread through droplets in the air and enters the maternal respiratory tract. Entry takes place and the virus grows in local lymphoid tissues, quickly spreading to the spleen. One week after the initial entry, there is viraemic spread to the respiratory tract, skin, kidneys and joints and if the subject is pregnant infection of the placenta can take place. The subject develops fever, tiredness and a maculopapular rash with enlarged lymph nodes 14-21 days after the initial entry.

Therefore, rubella virus has reached the placenta once the pregnant woman exhibits symptoms and signs.

The diagnosis of rubella is determined by showing the presence of rubella specific IgM in serum. The presence of rubella specific IgM in cord blood confirms that the fetus was exposed to rubella in utero.

What are the ways in which the baby can be affected by congenital rubella infection?

Rubella is capable of causing; microcephaly, mental handicap, cataracts, nerve deafness, myocarditis, cardiac malformations especially atrio-ventricular septal defect, enlarged liver, enlarged spleen and haematological disorders such as anaemia and thrombocytopoenia. Rubella has anti-mitotic actions. The total number of cells in a baby with congenital rubella is reduced. This would contribute to the risks of low birth weight and growth restriction. Cell mediated immune responses to rubella are delayed in infants exposed to rubella in early pregnancy. The fetus does produce IgM to the virus but cell mediated responses can take years to develop. After birth, an infected baby harbours live rubella virus in the throat, urine, brain and eye.

Consider these 2 MCQs;

Rubella

A. Is a DNA virus   **False**

B. Is a cause of multi-organ failure in previously healthy adults   **False**

C. Has an incubation period of one week in adults   **False**

D. Always causes congenital infection when a pregnant woman is exposed during the first trimester   **False**

E. May be diagnosed by demonstrating the presence of specific IgM in serum   **True**

An infant with congenital rubella infection;

A. Is at risk of mental handicap   **True**

B. May have purpura   **True**

C. Is likely to be large for dates   **False**

D. May infect susceptible individuals   **True**

E. Must be treated with antiviral drugs if malformations are present   **False**

Consider this EMQ;

A. Attenuation
B. Chemical mutagenesis
C. DNA vaccination
D. Gene cloning
E. Synthesis of immunoglobulin
F. Toxoid preparation

In order to produce a live vaccine to rubella scientists infected living rabbit kidney cells in vitro with a live sample of the virus. The cells divided and the rubella virus passed through several cell lines. Random mutation of the rubella virus occurred and selected mutants with lower virulence were used to produce a vaccine. Select the method of production of this type of vaccine from the list of options.

Answer –A

References

Brunton LL, Lazo JS, Parker KL. Goodman & Gilman's: The Pharmacological basis of Therapeutics, 11th edn. New York: McGraw-Hill Company; 2006

Devlin TM. Textbook of biochemistry with Clinical Correlations, 6th edn. Hoboken, NJ: Wiley-Liss; 2006

Duthie J, Hodges P. EMQs for the MRCOG Part 1, 1st edn. London: RCOG; 2007

Duthie J, Hodges P. EMQs for the MRCOG Part 2, 1st edn. London: RCOG; 2006

England N. Physics Matters, 3rd edn. London: Hodder & Stoughton Educational; 2001

Guyton AC, Hall JE. Textbook of Medical Physiology, 11th edn. Philadelphia, Pennsylvania: Elsevier Inc.; 2006

Johnston TB, Whillis J. Gray's Anatomy: Descriptive and Applied, 3rd edn. London: Longmans Green and Co. Ltd; 1949

Larsen WJ. Human Embryology, 1st edn. New York: Churchill Livingstone; 1993

Mims C, Dockrell HM, Goering RV, Roitt I, Wakelin D, Zuckerman M. Medical Microbiology, 4th edn. Edinburgh: Elsevier Linited, 2004

Pritchard DJ, Korf BR. Medical Genetics at a Glance, 2nd edn. Oxford: Blackwell Publishing; 2008

Protection of air, crew from cosmic radiation: Guidance material, Department for Transport www.dft.gov.uk/pgr/aviation/hio/protectionofaircrewfromcosmi296/

Reece EA, Hobbins JC, Mahoney MJ, Petrie RH. Medicine of the Fetus & Mother, 1st edn. Philadelphia, Pennsylvania: J. B. Lippincott Company; 1992

Swiet MD, Chamberlain G, Bennett P. Basic Science in Obstetrics and Gynaecology, 3d edn. Edinburgh: Churchill Livingstone; 2002

Underwood JCE. General and Systematic pathology, 4th edn. Edinburgh: Churchill Livingstone; 2004

Full Specimen Examination Paper 1

EMQ SECTION

Options

A Accessory obturator nerve
B First lumbar nerve
C Obturator nerve
D Pudendal nerve
E Sciatic nerve
F Superior gluteal nerve

Instructions

The list of options contains the names of different nerves which give rise to branches. For each nerve in the items below select the nerve from which it arises. Each option may be used once, more than once or not at all.

Question 1   Iliohypogastric nerve

Question 2   Ilio-inguinal nerve

Options

A External pudendal nerve
B Genitofemoral nerve
C Internal pudendal nerve
D Obturator nerve
E Pudendal nerve
F Sciatic nerve

Question 3 The pelvic part of the ureter descends along the anterior border of the greater sciatic notch under cover of the peritoneum. The ureter lies in front of the internal iliac artery, medial to the middle rectal, inferior vesical and obturator arteries and which one of the nerves in the list of options?

Options

A   Abdominal aorta
B   Azygos arteries of the vagina
C   Common iliac artery
D   External iliac artery
E   Inferior vesical artery
F   Internal iliac artery
G   Obturator artery
H   Ovarian artery
I   Superior vesical artery
J   Uterine artery

Instructions

The list of options contains the names of different arteries. For each of the items below select the single most likely vessel from the list of options. Each option may be used once, more than once or not at all.

Question 4   The pelvic part of the ureter descends on the anterior border of the greater sciatic notch, under cover of the peritoneum and lies in front of which one of the arteries in the list of options?

Options

A   Bilateral renal agenesis

B   Congenital cystic adenomatoid malformation of the lung

C   Congenital diaphragmatic hernia

D   Dextrocardia

E   Malrotation of the mid-gut

F   Pulmonary hypoplasia

G   Situs inversus

H   Tracheo-oesophageal fistula

Instructions

Select the single most likely outcome for each of the embryological processes described in the items below. Each option may be used once, more than once or not at all.

Question 5   At the beginning of the fifth week a pair of transverse membranes form between the root of the twelfth rib and the tips of the seventh to twelfth ribs. The membrane on the left fails to form completely and there is failure to fuse with the septum transversum.

Options

A   Bulbus cordis→ conotruncus→ primitive atrium→
    ventricle→ sinus venosus

B   Bulbus cordis→ conotruncus→ sinus venosus→
    ventricle→ primitive atrium

C   Conotruncus→ bulbus cordis→ sinus venosus→
    ventricle→ primitive atrium

D   Conotruncus→ bulbus cordis→ ventricle→
    primitive atrium → sinus venosus

E   Sinus venosus→ primitive atrium→ ventricle→
    bulbus cordis→ conotruncus

F   Sinus venosus→ primitive atrium→ ventricle→
    conotruncus→ bulbus cordis

G   Ventricle→ bulbus cordis→ conotruncus→
    primitive atrium→ sinus venosus

H   Ventricle→ bulbus cordis→ conotruncus→
    sinus venosus→ primitive atrium

Question 6   The human heart forms as a tubular structure
in early life which receives blood from the
umbilical, cardinal and vitelline veins. The blood
flows through the primitive heart and leaves at
the cephalic end. From the list of options select
the single most correct sequence of blood flow
through the different parts of the heart from
caudal inflow to cephalic outflow.

Options

A   Alpha feto protein
B   Human chorionic gonadotrophin
C   Human placental lactogen
D   Inhibin A
E   Inhibin B
F   Oestriol
G   Oestrone
H   Progesterone
I   Testosterone

Instructions

Select the single most likely match for each of the substances described in the items below from the list of options. Each option may be used once, more than once or not at all.

Question 7   The substance is produced in the fetal liver and has a molecular structure similar to that of albumin. However, antibodies raised against the substance had very little cross reactivity with albumin. The level of the substance is comparatively low in fetuses with trisomy 21.

Question 8   The substance is a glycoprotein with a molecular weight of about 39,000. Its level in a pregnant woman's serum can first be measured about 9 days following ovulation and soon after the blastocyst implants in the endometrium. Under the influence of the substance the corpus luteum enlarges to twice its initial size over the first month of pregnancy.

Options

A   Achondroplasia
B   Acromegaly
C   Conn syndrome
D   Cushing syndrome
E   Diabetes insipidus
F   Osteopetrosis
G   Osteomalacia
H   Osteoporosis

Instructions

For each of the endocrine disorders described in the items below select the single most likely diagnosis from the list of options. Each option may be used once, more than once or not at all.

Question 9   The secretion of a certain polypeptide hormone was increased as a result of an adenoma affecting the eosinophil cells of the anterior pituitary. The hormone attached to specific receptors on the surface of cells in different sites in the body. The effects included enlarged hands and feet, enlargement of the heart and liver, hypertension and elevation of serum glucose.

Question 10   The secretion of a certain polypeptide hormone was increased as a result of an adenoma affecting the basophil cells of the anterior pituitary. The effects were bilateral adrenocortical hyperplasia and increased urinary excretion of 17-hydroxysteroids.

Options

A   Coxsackie A
B   Cytomegalovirus
C   Echovirus
D   Hepatitis B virus
E   Human erythrovirus B19
F   Measles
G   Mumps
H   Rubella
I   Smallpox
J   Varicella zoster virus

Instructions   The list of options contains the name of different types of viruses. The items below describe the biological behaviour of certain viruses in human infection. Select the single most likely cause from the list of options for the scenarios in the items below. Each option may be used once, more than once or not at all.

Question 11   The double stranded DNA virus was morphologically similar to herpes simplex virus. The virus was present in the respiratory secretions of an infected child. Upon sneezing, droplets containing the virus spread into the air and were inhaled by a susceptible human. The virus crossed the surface epithelium in the respiratory tract and infected mononuclear cells. The infected cells carried the virus to lymphoid tissues and over the next week the organism multiplied within mononuclear cells. Then, the infected mononuclear cells containing the virus spread the organism to epithelial sites; the respiratory tract, skin over the trunk, face and scalp. The virus produced characteristic lesions at these sites about 14 days after the initial infection. Multinucleated giant cells with intra-nuclear inclusions were present at the sites of epithelial infection.

Question 12 A pregnant woman became infected with a RNA virus through her respiratory tract. The virus replicated in local lymphoid issues and then spread to other lymph nodes and the spleen. One week after the initial entry the woman developed viraemia. The virus infected the skin to produce a maculopapular rash and infected the respiratory tract and placenta. The fetus was also infected and developed anomalies of the heart and nervous system.

Options

A   Bacillus anthracis
B   Bacillus cereus
C   Clostridium botulinum
D   Clostridium difficile
E   Clostridium tetani
F   Escheridia coli
G   Francisella tularensis
H   Leptospira interrogans
I   Shigella dysenteriae
J   Yersinia pestis

Question 13 An otherwise healthy woman developed a wound infection as the result of trauma sustained while working with soil. Gram negative bacilli multiplied rapidly in the wound and produced an exotoxin. The exotoxin caused muscular spasm and respiratory difficulty. Select the single most likely causative organism from the list of options.

Options

A   B-lactamase
B   Biliverdin reductase
C   Hexosaminidase A
D   Lactase
E   Sphingomyelinase
F   Tyrosine kinase

Question 14   Clavulanic acid binds irreversibly to which one of the enzymes in the list of options?

Options

A   Ampicillin
B   Cefuroxime
C   Chloramphenicol
D   Gentamicin
E   Methicillin
F   Tetracycline
G   Trimethoprim

Instructions

Select the single most likely antibiotic from the list of options which would account for the side effects described in the items below. Each option may be used once, more than once or not at all.

Question 15   A woman received parenteral treatment with the antibiotic for several days. Serum levels of the drug were not monitored. The drug was accumulated in the proximal renal tubule and led to excretion of enzymes of the renal tubular brush border. Then, the woman developed mild proteinuria and there were hyaline and granular casts in the urine.

Question 16   A pregnant woman was given the antibiotic in tablet form and it was not realised that she was pregnant. The antibiotic entered the fetal circulation and was deposited in the developing bones and teeth as an antibiotic-calcium orthophosphate complex. Some time after birth it was noted that the child had discoloured teeth.

Options

A   0.0035
B   0.028
C   0.035
D   0.35
E   1
F   1.28
G   2.8
H   3.5

Instructions   The coefficient of variation is sometimes used to assess the reliability of clinical measurements. The list of options contains different values for the coefficient of variation. For each of the scenarios described below select the single most correct coefficient of variation from the list of options. Each option may be used once, more than once or not at all.

Question 17   As a component of an exercise in quality control, an Obstetric department asked 100 different Doctors and midwives to measure the symphysis-fundal distance in the same pregnant woman. The woman was 28 weeks pregnant, the mean of the 100 measurements was 28 cm and the standard deviation was 1cm. Select the coefficient of variation from the list of options.

Question 18   As a component of an exercise in quality control, an Obstetric department asked 100 different Doctors and midwives to measure the symphysis-fundal distance in the same pregnant woman. The woman was 28 weeks pregnant, the mean of the 100 measurements was 28 cm and 95% of the measurements were between 26cm and 30cm. Select the coefficient of variation from the list of options.

Options

A   69-70Kg

B   69.2-70.2Kg

C   69.3-71Kg

D   69.4-70Kg

E   69.4-70.6Kg

F   70-70.3Kg

G   70-70.6Kg

H   70.6-71.3Kg

Instructions   Confidence intervals are used to describe the distribution of data in a certain sample. For each of the sets of data presented in the items below select the single most correct 95% confidence interval for the mean from the list of options. Each option may be used once, more than once or not at all.

Question 19   The weights of 1,000 pregnant women were reliably measured. The mean weight was 70 Kg and the standard error of the mean was 0.3 Kg.

Question 20   The weights of 1,000 pregnant women were reliably measured. The mean weight was 70 Kg and the standard deviation was 9.3Kg.

Full Specimen Examination Paper 1

MCQ SECTION

All question items 21-68,
A to E inclusive, to be answered TRUE or FALSE.

Question 21 The right ventricle in the normal adult heart;

A   Is derived from the bulbus cordis
B   Is well innervated by sympathetic nerves
C   Is well innervated by Vagal nerve endings
D   Contracts at the same time as the left atrium in a normal cardiac cycle
E   Receives oxygenated blood from the pulmonary veins

Question 22 The internal pudendal artery in the adult woman gives rise to the following;

A   Deep artery of the clitoris
B   Lateral sacral arteries
C   Inferior rectal artery
D   Inferior vesical artery
E   Descending genicular artery

Question 23 The pineal gland;

A   Lies between the superior colliculi
B   Is 8 cm in length
C   Has a poor blood supply
D   Is more active during the hours of darkness
E   Is absent in the early human embryo

Question 24 The pudendal nerve;

A   Is derived from the ventral divisions of the second, third and fourth sacral ventral rami
B   Leaves the pelvis via the greater sciatic foramen
C   Lies between the piriformis and coccygeous muscles as it leaves the pelvis
D   Crosses the sacrospinous ligament
E   Lies lateral to the internal pudendal artery

Question 25 The lymphatic drainage of the vulva includes the;

A   Rectal lymphatic plexus
B   Deep femoral nodes
C   Popliteal nodes
D   Superficial inguinal nodes
E   Deep inguinal nodes

Question 26 The endometrial stroma contains;

A   Blood vessels
B   Lymph vessels
C   Parasympathetic nerves
D   Sympathetic nerves
E   Nabothian cysts

Question 27 The squamo-columnar junction of the cervix;

A   Varies in position with age
B   Usually recedes into the endocervical canal in pregnant women
C   Is the junction between the columnar secretory epithelium of the endocervical canal and the stratified squamous epithelium covering the ectocervix
D   Is characterised by Nabothian cysts
E   Is the site of all malignant disease in the cervix

Question 28 The round ligament;

A   Is approximately 12 cm long in an adult non-pregnant woman
B   Contains the processus vaginalis in fetal life
C   Passes across the internal iliac vessels
D   Enters the deep inguinal ring at the start of the inferior epigastric artery
E   Is inserted into the labia minora

Question 29 The diaphragm;

A   Receives its sensory nerve supply from the phrenic nerve
B   Has a convex lower surface
C   Transmits the thoraxic duct at the level of the twelfth thoraxic vertebra
D   Is maximal in height when the body is supine
E   Performs the largest respiratory excursions with normal breathing when the body is supine

Question 30 The pelvic splanchnic nerves;

A   Arise from the anterior primary rami of the second, third and fourth sacral nerves
B   Contain both parasympathetic and sympathetic fibres
C   Contribute to the pelvic plexus
D   Are similar in diameter to the sciatic nerve
E   Are preganglionic and medullated

Question 31 Concerning the human embryo at the third week of development (one week after first missed menstrual period);

A   The embryo is 4mm long
B   The primitive streak appears
C   There are 2 germ layers
D   The cardiovascular system begins to develop
E   The gonads are present

Question 32 Concerning the early human embryo;

A   The notochord induces the overlying ectoderm to form the neural tube
B   The paraxial mesoderm gives rise to the urogenital system
C   The paraxial mesoderm gives rise to the axial skeleton
D   The rapid growth of the brain leads to longitudinal folding of the embryo
E   Enlargement of the somites leads to lateral folding

Question 33 Concerning the embryological development of the urinary tract;

A   The urogenital sinus forms the vestibule of the vagina in females
B   The urogenital sinus forms the penile urethra in males
C   The urogenital sinus forms the trigone of the bladder in both males and females
D   The kidneys ascend from their original sacral site to a lumbar site between the sixth and ninth weeks
E   Renal neurons arise from cells of the neural crest

Question 34 The rhombencephalon gives rise to;

A   The eyes
B   The medulla oblongata
C   The cerebellum
D   The ciliary ganglion
E   Rathke's pouch

Question 35 Trophoblast;

A   Produces syncytiotrophoblast which secretes hydrolytic enzymes
B   Is the main source of alpha feto protein
C   Gives rise to decidual cells which then form the placenta
D   Actively transports nutrients into the blastocyst
E   Contains germ cells

Question 36 Concerning human metabolism of iodine;

A Saltwater fish is a good dietary source
B About 20% of circulating iodides are selectively absorbed by cells in the thyroid gland
C Iodides must be oxidised before combining with tyrosine
D Thiocyanate competitively inhibits the transport of iodine into the thyroid cell
E The presence of high levels of plasma iodides increases the size and blood supply of the thyroid gland

Question 37 Testosterone;

A Contains 21 atoms of carbon in each molecule
B Is a major secretory product in the Leydig cells of the testes
C Is converted to dihydrotestosterone by the action of aromatase
D Is converted to oestradiol by the action of 5α-reductase
E Loosely binds to plasma albumin

Question 38 Sex hormone binding globulin

A Is a beta globulin
B Is produced in the renal juxtaglomerular apparatus
C Binds testosterone with a greater affinity than oestradiol
D Levels are elevated in hyperthyroidism
E Levels are elevated in polycystic ovarian syndrome

Question 39 The posterior lobe of the pituitary gland;

A Is formed from the infundibulum which is a diverticulum of the diencephalic floor

B Contains glial like cells

C Secretes growth hormone

D Synthesises antidiuretic hormone

E Releases oxytocin

Question 40 Oxytocin;

A Is a polypeptide molecule which contains 9 amino acids

B Is synthesised by the ovaries during pregnancy

C Release is stimulated by the suckling response in a lactating woman

D Is associated with an increase in the biosynthesis of testosterone in males

E Is degraded by oxytocin transhydrogenase

Question 41 Parathyroid hormone;

A Is produced in the parathyroid glands

B Is derived from cholesterol

C Has a half life of 24 hours

D Increases plasma calcium

E Decreases plasma phosphate

Question 42 The following conditions may cause secondary amenorrhoea;

A Androgen insensitivity syndrome
B Anorexia nervosa
C Polycystic ovarian syndrome
D Primary ovarian failure
E Pelvic tuberculosis

Question 43 Steroid hormone receptors;

A Function as ligand dependent transcription factors
B Act in the nucleus of target cells when activated
C Contain a dimerization domain
D Contain a RNA binding domain
E Interact with enzymes that can affect gene transcription

Question 44 Follicle stimulating hormone;

A Is a lipoprotein
B Is biosynthesised in the pre-optic area of the hypothalamus
C Binds to receptors on the nuclear membranes of the cells of the ovarian follicle
D Is capable of binding to receptors for thyroid stimulating hormone
E Is similar in structure to oestradiol

Question 45 Prolactin;

A Is a single chain polypeptide
B Is produced in the anterior lobe of the pituitary gland
C Has a molecular weight of 22,000
D Causes differentiation of secretory cells in the breast
E Stimulates synthesis of components of milk

Question 46 Concerning infections affecting the nervous system;

A Cerebral malaria accounts for fewer than 10,000 deaths per annum on a global scale
B Clostridium tetanus toxin causes overactivity of motor neurones
C Toxocara infection can cause granuloma formation in the brain
D Toxoplasmosis can cause intracranial calcification
E Clostridium botulinum toxin blocks acetylcholine release within the central nervous system

Question 47 Concerning Cytomegalovirus;

A There is only one serotype
B Sexual contact may enable spread
C Sensitivity to penicillin is a unique feature
D It is capable of producing mental handicap following transplacental fetal infection
E The infection is controlled by cell mediated immunity

Question 48 Chlamydia trachomatis;

A Exists as an elementary body adapted for extracellular survival

B Exists as a reticulate body adapted for intracellular multiplication

C Has only one serotype

D May produce an ocular infection

E Is sensitive to metronidazole

Question 49 Endotoxins;

A Are characteristically released by gram negative bacteria

B Are typically lipopolysaccharides

C Induce fever

D May lead to septic shock

E Are a by product of actively dividing cells

Question 50 The following organisms secrete exotoxin;

A Clostridium tetani

B Bacillus anthracis

C Neisseria meningitidis

D Staphylococcus aureus

E Plasmodium ovale

Question 51 Toxoplasma gondii is sensitive to;

A Pyrimethamine
B Pyridoxine
C Metronidazole
D Sulfadiazine
E Spiramycin

Question 52 Trichomonas vaginalis;

A May be observed as a motile trophozoite on microscopic examination of material from a high vaginal swab taken from an infected woman
B Forms clue cells
C Leads to an increase in the vaginal pH
D Has a worldwide distribution
E Forms colonies on solid culture media

Question 53 Low molecular weight heparins;

A May be taken orally
B Cross the placenta
C Are associated with a lower incidence of thrombocytopoenia than standard heparin
D Are isolated from standard heparin by gel filtration chromatography
E Are identical with each other in their mechanism of action

Question 54 Warfarin;

A   Is usually detectable in plasma within one hour of oral intake
B   Is bound to albumin
C   Has a half life of 30 minutes
D   Decreases the international normalised ratio (INR)
E   Is excreted unchanged in the urine

Question 55 The following increase the risk of haemorrhage in a woman taking warfarin;

A   Clopidogrel
B   Carbemazepine
C   Sodium valproate
D   Fluoxetine
E   Nephrotic syndrome

Question 56 Raloxifene;

A   Is a testosterone receptor blocking agent
B   Is taken orally
C   Is an oestrogen agonist in bone
D   Causes endometrial proliferation
E   Is metabolised in the liver

Question 57 Progesterone;

A   Undergoes first pass metabolism
B   Is bound by albumin in plasma
C   Is metabolised to pregnane-3α,20α-diol
D   Produces endometrial proliferation
E   Decreases uterine contractility

Question 58 Nitrous oxide given as an inhalational agent;

A   Is a weak anaesthetic agent
B   Is highly soluble in blood
C   Selectively dilates the pulmonary arteries
D   May increase cerebral blood flow
E   Is nephrotoxic

Question 59 The following drugs inhibit the activity of platelets;

A   Salicylic acid
B   Clopidogrel
C   Dipyridamole
D   Aminocaproic acid
E   Abciximab

Question 60 The following anti-neoplastic agents form adducts with DNA;

A   Alkylating agents
B   Gemcitabine
C   6-mercaptopurine
D   Cis-platinum
E   Paclitaxel

Question 61 A clinical trial may not represent the true difference between 2 groups for the following reasons;

A Selection bias
B Exclusion bias after randomisation
C Distortion by an unpredictable factor
D Inadequate numbers
E Result produced as a random chance

Question 62 The following tests are applied to data with a normal distribution;

A One sample t-test
B Two sample t-test
C Paired t-test
D Wilcoxon matched pairs signed rank-sum test
E Wilcoxon rank-sum test

Question 63 A study on changes in maternal weight was carried out and the measurements in Kg were as follows; 1,1,2,2,2,3,5,8,10,18,25. The following statements can be made;

A The median is 5
B The average is 5
C The mode is 2
D The range is 10
E Measurements between 5 and 18 occurred by chance

Question 64   In a normal distribution;

A   The parameter which is being measured is plotted on the "y" axis

B   The number of subjects with a certain measurement is plotted on the "x" axis

C   There is a single peak at the centre

D   The mean and mode are exactly the same

E   The median is at a distance of one standard error from the mean

Question 65   The following properties of a screening test are explained as follows;

A   The sensitivity provides information on the number of cases that were actually detected

B   A low level of specificity ensures that the test is acceptable

C   The specificity divided by the sensitivity is the likelihood ratio

D   The positive predictive value is a measure of the probability that a person testing screen positive actually has the condition

E   A high number of false positives would increase the positive predictive value

Question 66   In a study with a p value;

A   The smaller the p value, the stronger the evidence against the null hypothesis

B   The greater the p value, the stronger the evidence for the null hypothesis

C   The p value measures the strength of evidence for a difference

D   The p value is entirely independent of sample size

E   The p value provides accurate information on the size of a difference

Question 67 A maternity unit had the following vital statistics; 5,000 total births, 20 late fetal losses, 10 stillbirths due to an identified cause, 10 unexplained stillbirths, 30 neonatal deaths during the first week of life, 10 neonatal deaths during the second, third and fourth week of life and there were 2 maternal deaths. Of the total of 40 neonatal deaths prematurity accounted for 30 deaths. From this information the following may be deduced;

A The perinatal mortality rate was 10 per thousand total births

B There were 10 stillbirths due to congenital malformations

C The most common cause of perinatal loss was prematurity

D There is no data on birth weight specific perinatal loss

E Both maternal deaths were avoidable

Question 68 In a normal distribution curve;

A The number of values above the mode is the same as the number of values below it

B The spread of the curve is described by the standard deviation

C The interquartile range contains 25 % of the observations

D The 50th percentile is the median

E 75 % of the observations are greater than the 75th percentile

Full Specimen Examination Paper 2

EMQ SECTION

Options

A   Folic acid
B   Vitamin A
C   Vitamin B_
D   Vitamin B2
E   Vitamin B6
F   Vitamin B12
G   Vitamin C
H   Vitamin D
I   Vitamin E
J   Vitamin K

Instructions   Select the single most likely substance from the list of options that accounts for the scenarios described in the items below. Each option may be used once, more than once or not at all.

Question 1   The substance is a precursor to a co-enzyme which is critical to certain steps in the citric acid cycle and the pentose phosphate pathway. It is also a precursor to another substance which appears to function in the transmission of nerve impulses. Severe deficiency leads to compensatory peripheral vasodilatation, reduced total peripheral resistance and a marked rise in cardiac output. There is also weakness of the muscles and unsteady gait.

Question 2   The substance is required for the conversion of glutamic acid residues to γ-carboxyglutamic acid residues in certain proteins. The γ-carboxyglutamic acid residues allow prothrombin to bind calcium ions and the prothrombin-calcium complex binds to the negatively charged phospholipid surfaces of platelets and endothelial cells at the site of an injury.

Question 3   The deficiency of the substance inhibits synthesis of DNA by decreasing the availability of purines and dTMP. The clinical effects include macrocytic anaemia and an increased risk of cancer of the colon. In pregnant women a deficiency of the substance increases the risk of neural tube defect in the baby.

Options

A   Allosteric control
B   Compartmentation
C   Competitive inhibition
D   Cross regulation
E   Negative feedback inhibition
F   Positive feedback inhibition

Question 4   The biosynthesis of fatty acids generally takes place in the cytoplasm of the human cell and the oxidation of fatty acids takes place inside the mitochondria. The reactions are separated by the mitochondrial membrane. Select the single most correct term from the list of options for this phenomenon.

Options

A   Alpha radiation
B   Electron beams
C   Gamma radiation
D   Kilo-voltage X rays
E   Mega-voltage X rays
F   Positron radiation

Instructions   For each of the types of radiation described in the items below, select the single most correct type of radiation from the list of options. Each option may be used once, more than once or not at all.

Question 5   Cobalt 60 is used as the source of radiation and the beam has a high penumbra

Question 6   Electromagnetic radiation used in diagnostic radiology

Question 7   A linear accelerator is used to direct electrons onto a target which then emits electromagnetic radiation with a narrow penumbra and a precise beam

Options

A   Augmentation
B   Capacitation
C   Fractionation
D   Neutralisation
E   Palliation

Question 8   A woman undergoes radiotherapy for invasive carcinoma of the cervix. Repeated doses of teletherapy to the pelvis are applied. The doses used are moderate and the aim is to deliver a higher total dose of radiation than would be possible with a single dose. Select the single most correct term for this regimen from the list of options.

Options

A   Achondroplasia
B   Congenital adrenal hyperplasia
C   Down syndrome
D   Fragile X syndrome
E   Marfan syndrome
F   Phenylketonuria
G   Neurofibromatosis type 1
H   Neurofibromatosis type 2

Instructions   Select the single most likely genetic disorder which would result from the mutations described in the items below. Each option may be used once, more than once or not at all.

Question 9   The mutation affected the genes coding for fibroblast growth factor receptor 3 (FGFR 3) expressed in chondrocytes. As a result there was premature differentiation of chondrocytes into bone. The affected individual had severe shortening of the proximal segments of all 4 limbs. There was no family history of an individual affected by the same disorder.

Question 10   A mutant protein bound to and disabled normal fibrillin-1. As a result the individual developed long, slender limbs and fingers and pectus excavatum. The cardiac defects included dilatation of the aortic root and mitral valve prolapse. There was a strong family of individuals affected by the same disorder.

Question 11   In an individual with a karyotype 46XY, there was an unstable length mutation in the FMR1 gene on the X chromosome. The increase in the length of the chromosome was beyond a critical size and the individual developed learning difficulties.

Options

A   Haem
B   Purine
C   Pyrimidine
D   Urea
E   Tyrosine
F   Sphingolipid
G   Heparan sulphate
H   Glycogen

Instructions   The list of options contains different metabolites. The items below refer to different metabolic disorders which lead to abnormal biosynthetic pathways involving specific metabolites. Select the metabolite which is most likely to be affected in each of the items below. Each option may be used once, more than once or not at all.

Question 12   Acute intermittent porphyria

Question 13   Occulocutaneous albinism

Question 14   Ocular albinism

Options

A   6.8

B   7.0

C   7.2

D   7.4

E   7.6

F   7.8

G   8.0

H   8.2

Instructions   The list of options contains different values for Ph. For each item below select the single most likely pH from the list of options. Each option may be used once, more than once or not at all.

Question 15   An understanding of placental transfer of drugs is of fundamental importance. Owing to a difference between fetal and maternal pH ion trapping of basic drugs occurs. What is the pH of fetal plasma?

Question 16   What is the pH of the plasma in a normal healthy pregnant woman?

Options

A Anaphase
B Cytokinesis
C Metaphase
D Pro-metaphase
E Prophase
F Telophase

Instructions The list of options contains different phases of the cell cycle. The items below describe critical events in the cell cycle. For each item below select the single most correct phase in the cell cycle from the list of options. Each option may be used once, more than once or not at all.

Question 17 Chromosomes align midway between the poles of the spindles creating a plate.

E
M
Q
2

Options

A   Adrenal blood flow

B   Adrenal plasma flow

C   Aortic blood flow

D   Colloid osmotic pressure

E   Glomerular filtration pressure

F   Glomerular filtration rate

G   Intravascular volume

H   Pressure inside Bowman's capsule

Question 18   24 hour creatinine clearance is measured in different clinical settings. Select the single most closely matching physiological parameter which matches creatinine clearance from the list of options.

Options

A 140
B 145
C 150
D 155
E 160
F 165
G 170
H 175

Question 19 Knowledge of a pregnant woman's serum creatinine, urinary creatinine and urine volume may be used to calculate creatinine clearance. The list of options provides different values of creatinine clearance in ml/minute. A pregnant woman was admitted for assessment and the relevant values were; serum creatinine = 60 µmol/l, urine creatinine=10 mmol/l, urine volume in 24 hours= 1.44l. Select the single most closely matching value for creatinine clearance from the list of options.

E
M
Q
2

A Heart rate x left ventricular end diastolic filling
   pressure

B Heart rate x right ventricular end diastolic filling
   pressure

C Heart rate x stroke volume

D Heart rate x total peripheral resistance

E Left ventricular end diastolic filling pressure x left
   ventricular end diastolic volume

F Left ventricular end systolic filling pressure x left
   ventricular end diastolic filling volume

G Stroke volume

H Stroke volume x pulmonary blood flow

Question 20 Select the single most correct formula for cardiac
output from the list of options.

Full Specimen Examination Paper 2

MCQ SECTION

All question items 21-68, A to E inclusive, to be answered TRUE or FALSE.

Question 21 The physical components of the sodium-potassium pump consist of;

A A receptor site for sodium ions Na$^+$
B A receptor site for potassium ions K$^+$
C A receptor site for aldosterone
D 3 protein subunits
E A lipopolysaccharide

Question 22 Concerning cardiac muscle;

A The cells act as a syncytium
B The energy to contract is chiefly derived from the oxidative metabolism of fatty acids
C Pre-load corresponds to the end diastolic pressure
D After-load corresponds to the pressure in the artery leading from the ventricle
E A rise in the level of potassium in the plasma leads to increased contractility

Question 23 Faeces contains the following;

A Protein
B Indole
C Stercobilin
D Skatole
E Water

M
C
Q
2

Question 24 Glomerular filtration rate is reduced by;

A   Angiotensin II
B   Bradykinin
C   Decreased renal blood flow
D   Noradrenaline
E   Ureteric obstruction

Question 25 The serum level of the following would be expected to decrease in a normal pregnancy;

A   Albumin
B   Ionised calcium
C   Total calcium
D   Vitamin B12
E   Zinc

Question 26 The serum level of the following would be expected to rise in a normal pregnancy;

A   FSH
B   Cortisol binding globulin
C   Glucose
D   Growth hormone
E   Thyroid binding globulin

Question 27 The nucleolus of the cell is associated with the following functions;

A   Synthesis of RNA
B   Processing of RNA
C   Synthesis of DNA
D   Synthesis of ribosomes
E   Cell motility

Question 28 Mitochondria are associated with the following functions;

A   Fatty acid elongation
B   Synthesis of proteins
C   Synthesis of DNA
D   Synthesis of RNA
E   Production of adenosine triphosphate (ATP)

Question 29 The volume of extracellular fluid in elevated in;

A   Adrenal insufficiency
B   Excessive production of antidiuretic hormone (ADH)
C   Cushing syndrome
D   Primary hyperaldosteronism
E   Diabetes insipidus

Question 30 Nitric oxide synthase II (iNOS) is induced by;

A   Interferon γ
B   Immunoglobulin G (IgG)
C   Tumour necrosis factor-α
D   Interleukin 1
E   Endotoxin

Question 31 Lysosomes;

A   Are derived from the Golgi apparatus
B   Have a diameter of 100 nanometres
C   Have a lipid trilayer membrane
D   Contain hydrolytic enzymes
E   Contain lysoferrin

M
C
Q
2

Question 32 Ciliary movement is observed in the following sites;

A   Bone marrow
B   Surface of the respiratory airways
C   Inside surface of the Fallopian tubes
D   Oesophageal lining
E   Hymen

Question 33 An alpha particle;

A   Is identical to the nucleus of a helium atom
B   Contains 2 protons and one neutron
C   Is positively charged
D   Is usually emitted by very heavy radioactive elements
E   May travel several metres through air following emission

Question 34 Cobalt 60;

A   Contains 60 protons within its nucleus
B   Emits gamma radiation
C   Is a gas at a temperature of 20 degrees Celsius
D   Has a half life of 5 years
E   May be used appropriately to kill bacteria in surgical instruments

A   Energy is carried by oscillating electric and magnetic forces

B   The electric force is at a right angle to the direction in which the wave travels

C   Cosmic radiation may cause gene mutations

D   The exposure to radiation for a woman travelling by air between the United Kingdom and Spain is approximately equivalent to five chest X-rays

E   Beta radiation is an example of electromagnetic radiation

Question 36 Concerning ionising radiation;

A   Alpha particles ionise air very strongly

B   Alpha particles possess the power to penetrate a lead shield which is 2cm in thickness

C   Beta particles ionise air more strongly than alpha particles

D   Beta particles can be deflected by a magnetic field

E   Gamma radiation can be deflected by a magnetic field

Question 37 The following conditions are causes of moderate and severe learning difficulties in children of school age;

A   Down syndrome

B   Edward syndrome

C   Fragile X syndrome

D   Cystic fibrosis

E   Tuberous sclerosis

M
C
Q
2

Question 38 Klinefelter syndrome;

A   Is diagnosed by the determination of the karyotype 47XYY

B   Is associated with male infertility

C   Is associated with severe learning difficulties in childhood

D   Can be diagnosed by ultrasound examination of the pelvis

E   Carries an increased risk of male breast cancer

Question 39 The following parameters are decreased in a pregnancy complicated by Down syndrome in the fetus;

A   Nuchal thickness

B   Free β-HCG in maternal serum

C   Total HCG in maternal serum

D   Pregnancy associated plasma protein A in maternal serum

E   Unconjugated oestriol in maternal urine

Question 40 A gene mutation is present in the fertilized human egg. Therefore the mutation will be transmitted to;

A   All the germ cells

B   All the somatic cells

C   Stem cells

D   Half the germ cells

E   25% of the somatic cells

Question 41 The following features would be expected in a baby with Edward syndrome;

A   Fetal macrosomy
B   Macrognathia
C   Cleft lip
D   Cleft palate
E   Fixed flexion deformities in the digits of the upper limb

Question 42 In an autosomal dominant condition;

A   Males are affected more commonly than females
B   A heterozygote may express the trait mildly
C   New mutations are common
D   If a person who is a heterozygote has a child with a person who does not have the gene, then the chance that the child will be affected is 100%
E   An affected man may transmit the condition to his daughter

Question 43 DNA replication requires;

A   DNA template
B   Primer with a free 3'-OH terminus
C   DNA polymerase
D   Helicases
E   Single stranded DNA binding proteins

M
C
Q
2

Question 44 tRNA;

A   Is a much larger molecule than mRNA

B   Has an amino acid acceptor stem at its 3' terminus

C   Acts as a carrier to transport its amino acid to the ribosome

D   Has a codon that interacts directly with the anticodon on mRNA

E   Lines up an amino acid in correct sequence to enable the formation of peptide bonds

Question 45 The following conditions can produce secondary immunodeficiency;

A   Crohn's disease

B   Nephrotic syndrome

C   Non Hodgkin's lymphoma

D   Severe combined immunodeficiency (SCID)

E   Splenectomy

Question 46 Selective IgA deficiency;

A   Has a prevalence of approximately 1 in 700 in the United Kingdom

B   Produces disease in 90% of those who are affected

C   Is transmitted as an autosomal dominant trait

D   Is associated with a serum IgG in the normal range

E   May be associated with an adverse reaction to blood transfusion

Question 47 The following are examples of pyogenic bacteria;

A   Chlamydia trachomatis
B   Clostridium difficile
C   Neisseria gonorrhoea
D   Streptococcus pyogenes
E   Staphylococcus aureus

Question 48 Cystic fibrosis;

A   Is caused by mutations of a gene in chromosome 8
B   Is transmitted as an autosomal dominant condition
C   Results due to abnormal encoding for a chloride channel in the nuclear membrane of epithelial cells
D   Is associated with viscid secretions
E   May lead to progressive bronchiectasis

Question 49 Meningiomas;

A   Are more common in women than in men
B   Arise from cells of the arachnoid cap
C   Commonly invade the brain
D   Lead to anatomical distortion of the brain
E   May contain psammoma bodies

M
C
Q
2

Question 50 Miliary tuberculosis;

A   Mar arise from primary tuberculosis

B   May arise from secondary tuberculosis

C   Is the widespread occurrence of small tuberculous granulomas in different organs

D   Is associated with an exaggerated response to the Mantoux test

E   Represents a medical emergency

Question 51 Tuberculous endometritis;

A   Occurs as a result of secondary spread

B   Never results in caseating granulomas

C   Is associated with the Arias-Stella phenomenon

D   Is diagnosed by the demonstration of alkali fast bacilli using the Ziehl Neelsen technique

E   Requires treatment with ionising radiation

Question 52 The following conditions may cause malformations of the central nervous system in the neonate;

A   Congenital cytomegalovirus infection

B   Down syndrome

C   Exposure to ionising radiation in utero

D   Fetal alcohol syndrome

E   Tuberous sclerosis

Question 53 Excess exposure to certain metals and chemical toxins may lead to toxicity affecting the nervous system. The following toxins are correctly paired with their recognised effects;

A   Aluminium – photosensitivity
B   Lead – encephalopathy in childhood
C   Manganese – degeneration of basal ganglia
D   Inorganic mercury - dementia
E   Organic mercury – optic nerve degeneration

Question 54 Multiple myeloma is associated with the following;

A   Onset of disease at puberty
B   Anaemia
C   Increased osteoclastic activity
D   Decreased blood viscosity
E   Bence Jones protein in the urine

Question 55 IgE;

A   Has a molecular weight of 200,000
B   Is embedded in the cell membrane of mast cells
C   Has 10 antigen binding sites
D   Is activated by complement
E   May be produced by B-lymphocytes

Question 56 The following are normal histological findings in liver tissue;

A   Hyaline globules
B   Mallory's hyalin
C   Kupffer cells
D   Granulomas
E   Space of Disse

Question 57 Histological examination of the liver shows portal tracts which contain branches of the;

A   Bile duct
B   Coeliac artery
C   Hepatic artery
D   Hepatic vein
E   Portal vein

Question 58 Concerning the process of healing at the site of a fractured bone;

A   Osteoblasts lay new bone
B   Fibroblasts are present
C   Islands of cartilage are sometimes present in the callus
D   Woven bone replaces lamellar bone
E   Lamellar bone replaces trabecular bone

Question 59 Gonadoblastoma;

A   Arise within streak gonads in individuals with a Y chromosome
B   Contain primitive germ cells
C   Contain Reinke's crystals
D   Undergoes malignant change to form dysgerminoma
E   Secretes human placental lactogen

Question 60 The following sites of bone marrow are involved in red blood cell production in the postmenopausal woman;

A   Femoral shaft
B   Ribs
C   Sternum
D   Tibial shaft
E   Vertebra

Question 61 The following enzymes are present in the mature red blood cell;

A   2,3-biphosphoglycerate mutase
B   Carbonic anhydrase
C   Glucose 6 phosphate dehydrogenase
D   Pyruvate kinase
E   Transketolase

Question 62 The following respiratory parameters are increased in a normal pregnancy;

A   Expiratory reserve volume
B   Forced expiratory volume
C   Peak expiratory flow rate
D   Minute volume
E   Carbon dioxide output

M
C
Q
2

Question 63 Acetylcholine;

A   Is synthesised from adrenaline and choline
B   Is held within a specific vesicle in the synapse
C   Is competitively inhibited by curare in nicotinic receptors
D   Is secreted at the terminals of large pyramidal cells from the motor cortex
E   Is absent in all postganglionic neurons of the sympathetic nervous system

Question 64 Nicotinic acetylcholine receptors (nAChR) are;

A   Ligand regulated channels
B   Pentameric complexes
C   Located in the post synaptic membrane
D   Inhibited by botulinum toxin
E   Inhibited by cobra toxin

Question 65 Dopamine;

A   Is a central neurotransmitter from the substantia nigra to the caudate nucleus and putamen
B   Is the metabolic precursor to noradrenaline
C   Is synthesised in the epithelial cells of the renal proximal tubule
D   Is highly effective if taken orally
E   Readily crosses the blood brain barrier

Question 66 The following structures are components of the sympathetic nervous system;

A   Coeliac ganglion
B   Ciliary ganglion
C   Hypogastric plexus
D   Occulomotor nerve
E   Vagus nerve

Question 67 The following cardiovascular changes are expected in a normal pregnancy;

A   Left ventricular dilatation
B   Left ventricular hypotrophy
C   Displacement of the apex of the heart to the left and pointing in a posterior direction
D   Right axis deviation in the electrocardiogram (ECG)
E   Ventricular tachycardia

Question 68 The following Vitamins are fat soluble;

A   Vitamin A
B   Vitamin C
C   Vitamin D
D   Vitamin E
E   Vitamin K

M
C
Q
2

EMQ Answer Paper 1

1 [A] [B] [C] [D] [E] [F] [G] [H] [I] [J] [K] [L] [M] [N] [O] [P] [Q] [R] [S] [T]
2 [A] [B] [C] [D] [E] [F] [G] [H] [I] [J] [K] [L] [M] [N] [O] [P] [Q] [R] [S] [T]
3 [A] [B] [C] [D] [E] [F] [G] [H] [I] [J] [K] [L] [M] [N] [O] [P] [Q] [R] [S] [T]
4 [A] [B] [C] [D] [E] [F] [G] [H] [I] [J] [K] [L] [M] [N] [O] [P] [Q] [R] [S] [T]
5 [A] [B] [C] [D] [E] [F] [G] [H] [I] [J] [K] [L] [M] [N] [O] [P] [Q] [R] [S] [T]
6 [A] [B] [C] [D] [E] [F] [G] [H] [I] [J] [K] [L] [M] [N] [O] [P] [Q] [R] [S] [T]
7 [A] [B] [C] [D] [E] [F] [G] [H] [I] [J] [K] [L] [M] [N] [O] [P] [Q] [R] [S] [T]
8 [A] [B] [C] [D] [E] [F] [G] [H] [I] [J] [K] [L] [M] [N] [O] [P] [Q] [R] [S] [T]
9 [A] [B] [C] [D] [E] [F] [G] [H] [I] [J] [K] [L] [M] [N] [O] [P] [Q] [R] [S] [T]
10 [A] [B] [C] [D] [E] [F] [G] [H] [I] [J] [K] [L] [M] [N] [O] [P] [Q] [R] [S] [T]
11 [A] [B] [C] [D] [E] [F] [G] [H] [I] [J] [K] [L] [M] [N] [O] [P] [Q] [R] [S] [T]
12 [A] [B] [C] [D] [E] [F] [G] [H] [I] [J] [K] [L] [M] [N] [O] [P] [Q] [R] [S] [T]
13 [A] [B] [C] [D] [E] [F] [G] [H] [I] [J] [K] [L] [M] [N] [O] [P] [Q] [R] [S] [T]
14 [A] [B] [C] [D] [E] [F] [G] [H] [I] [J] [K] [L] [M] [N] [O] [P] [Q] [R] [S] [T]
15 [A] [B] [C] [D] [E] [F] [G] [H] [I] [J] [K] [L] [M] [N] [O] [P] [Q] [R] [S] [T]
16 [A] [B] [C] [D] [E] [F] [G] [H] [I] [J] [K] [L] [M] [N] [O] [P] [Q] [R] [S] [T]
17 [A] [B] [C] [D] [E] [F] [G] [H] [I] [J] [K] [L] [M] [N] [O] [P] [Q] [R] [S] [T]
18 [A] [B] [C] [D] [E] [F] [G] [H] [I] [J] [K] [L] [M] [N] [O] [P] [Q] [R] [S] [T]
19 [A] [B] [C] [D] [E] [F] [G] [H] [I] [J] [K] [L] [M] [N] [O] [P] [Q] [R] [S] [T]
20 [A] [B] [C] [D] [E] [F] [G] [H] [I] [J] [K] [L] [M] [N] [O] [P] [Q] [R] [S] [T]

EMQ Answer Paper 2

1 [A] [B] [C] [D] [E] [F] [G] [H] [I] [J] [K] [L] [M] [N] [O] [P] [Q] [R] [S] [T]
2 [A] [B] [C] [D] [E] [F] [G] [H] [I] [J] [K] [L] [M] [N] [O] [P] [Q] [R] [S] [T]
3 [A] [B] [C] [D] [E] [F] [G] [H] [I] [J] [K] [L] [M] [N] [O] [P] [Q] [R] [S] [T]
4 [A] [B] [C] [D] [E] [F] [G] [H] [I] [J] [K] [L] [M] [N] [O] [P] [Q] [R] [S] [T]
5 [A] [B] [C] [D] [E] [F] [G] [H] [I] [J] [K] [L] [M] [N] [O] [P] [Q] [R] [S] [T]
6 [A] [B] [C] [D] [E] [F] [G] [H] [I] [J] [K] [L] [M] [N] [O] [P] [Q] [R] [S] [T]
7 [A] [B] [C] [D] [E] [F] [G] [H] [I] [J] [K] [L] [M] [N] [O] [P] [Q] [R] [S] [T]
8 [A] [B] [C] [D] [E] [F] [G] [H] [I] [J] [K] [L] [M] [N] [O] [P] [Q] [R] [S] [T]
9 [A] [B] [C] [D] [E] [F] [G] [H] [I] [J] [K] [L] [M] [N] [O] [P] [Q] [R] [S] [T]
10 [A] [B] [C] [D] [E] [F] [G] [H] [I] [J] [K] [L] [M] [N] [O] [P] [Q] [R] [S] [T]
11 [A] [B] [C] [D] [E] [F] [G] [H] [I] [J] [K] [L] [M] [N] [O] [P] [Q] [R] [S] [T]
12 [A] [B] [C] [D] [E] [F] [G] [H] [I] [J] [K] [L] [M] [N] [O] [P] [Q] [R] [S] [T]
13 [A] [B] [C] [D] [E] [F] [G] [H] [I] [J] [K] [L] [M] [N] [O] [P] [Q] [R] [S] [T]
14 [A] [B] [C] [D] [E] [F] [G] [H] [I] [J] [K] [L] [M] [N] [O] [P] [Q] [R] [S] [T]
15 [A] [B] [C] [D] [E] [F] [G] [H] [I] [J] [K] [L] [M] [N] [O] [P] [Q] [R] [S] [T]
16 [A] [B] [C] [D] [E] [F] [G] [H] [I] [J] [K] [L] [M] [N] [O] [P] [Q] [R] [S] [T]
17 [A] [B] [C] [D] [E] [F] [G] [H] [I] [J] [K] [L] [M] [N] [O] [P] [Q] [R] [S] [T]
18 [A] [B] [C] [D] [E] [F] [G] [H] [I] [J] [K] [L] [M] [N] [O] [P] [Q] [R] [S] [T]
19 [A] [B] [C] [D] [E] [F] [G] [H] [I] [J] [K] [L] [M] [N] [O] [P] [Q] [R] [S] [T]
20 [A] [B] [C] [D] [E] [F] [G] [H] [I] [J] [K] [L] [M] [N] [O] [P] [Q] [R] [S] [T]

Paper 1
EMQ Answer Key

1 [A] **[B]** [C] [D] [E] [F] [G] [H] [I] [J] [K] [L] [M] [N] [O] [P] [Q] [R] [S] [T]
2 [A] **[B]** [C] [D] [E] [F] [G] [H] [I] [J] [K] [L] [M] [N] [O] [P] [Q] [R] [S] [T]
3 [A] [B] [C] **[D]** [E] [F] [G] [H] [I] [J] [K] [L] [M] [N] [O] [P] [Q] [R] [S] [T]
4 [A] [B] [C] [D] [E] **[F]** [G] [H] [I] [J] [K] [L] [M] [N] [O] [P] [Q] [R] [S] [T]
5 [A] [B] **[C]** [D] [E] [F] [G] [H] [I] [J] [K] [L] [M] [N] [O] [P] [Q] [R] [S] [T]
6 [A] [B] [C] [D] **[E]** [F] [G] [H] [I] [J] [K] [L] [M] [N] [O] [P] [Q] [R] [S] [T]
7 **[A]** [B] [C] [D] [E] [F] [G] [H] [I] [J] [K] [L] [M] [N] [O] [P] [Q] [R] [S] [T]
8 [A] **[B]** [C] [D] [E] [F] [G] [H] [I] [J] [K] [L] [M] [N] [O] [P] [Q] [R] [S] [T]
9 [A] [B] **[C]** [D] [E] [F] [G] [H] [I] [J] [K] [L] [M] [N] [O] [P] [Q] [R] [S] [T]
10 [A] [B] [C] **[D]** [E] [F] [G] [H] [I] [J] [K] [L] [M] [N] [O] [P] [Q] [R] [S] [T]
11 [A] [B] [C] [D] [E] [F] [G] [H] [I] **[J]** [K] [L] [M] [N] [O] [P] [Q] [R] [S] [T]
12 [A] [B] [C] [D] [E] [F] [G] **[H]** [I] [J] [K] [L] [M] [N] [O] [P] [Q] [R] [S] [T]
13 [A] [B] **[C]** [D] [E] [F] [G] [H] [I] [J] [K] [L] [M] [N] [O] [P] [Q] [R] [S] [T]
14 **[A]** [B] [C] [D] [E] [F] [G] [H] [I] [J] [K] [L] [M] [N] [O] [P] [Q] [R] [S] [T]
15 [A] [B] [C] **[D]** [E] [F] [G] [H] [I] [J] [K] [L] [M] [N] [O] [P] [Q] [R] [S] [T]
16 [A] [B] [C] [D] [E] **[F]** [G] [H] [I] [J] [K] [L] [M] [N] [O] [P] [Q] [R] [S] [T]
17 [A] [B] **[C]** [D] [E] [F] [G] [H] [I] [J] [K] [L] [M] [N] [O] [P] [Q] [R] [S] [T]
18 [A] [B] **[C]** [D] [E] [F] [G] [H] [I] [J] [K] [L] [M] [N] [O] [P] [Q] [R] [S] [T]
19 [A] [B] [C] [D] **[E]** [F] [G] [H] [I] [J] [K] [L] [M] [N] [O] [P] [Q] [R] [S] [T]
20 [A] [B] [C] [D] **[E]** [F] [G] [H] [I] [J] [K] [L] [M] [N] [O] [P] [Q] [R] [S] [T]

MCQ Answers

	A	B	C	D	E		A	B	C	D	E
21	T	T	F	F	F	45	T	T	T	T	T
22	T	F	T	F	F	46	F	T	T	T	F
23	T	F	F	T	F	47	T	T	F	T	T
24	T	T	T	T	F	48	T	T	F	T	F
25	T	T	F	T	T	49	T	T	T	T	F
26	T	T	T	T	F	50	T	T	F	T	F
27	T	F	T	F	F	51	T	F	F	T	T
28	T	T	F	T	F	52	T	F	T	T	F
29	F	F	T	T	T	53	F	F	T	T	F
30	T	F	T	F	T	54	T	T	F	F	F
31	T	T	F	T	F	55	T	F	T	T	F
32	T	F	T	T	T	56	F	T	T	F	T
33	T	T	F	T	T	57	T	T	T	F	T
34	F	T	T	F	F	58	T	F	F	T	F
35	T	F	F	T	F	59	T	T	T	F	T
36	T	T	T	T	F	60	T	F	F	T	F
37	F	T	F	F	T	61	T	T	T	T	T
38	T	F	T	T	F	62	T	T	T	F	F
39	T	T	F	F	T	63	F	F	T	F	F
40	T	F	T	T	T	64	F	T	T	T	F
41	T	F	F	T	T	65	T	F	F	T	F
42	F	T	T	T	T	66	T	T	T	F	F
43	T	T	T	F	T	67	T	F	T	T	F
44	F	F	F	F	F	68	T	T	F	T	F

Paper 2
EMQ Answer Key

Q	Answer	Q	Answer
1	[C]	11	[D]
2	[J]	12	[A]
3	[B]	13	[E]
4	[B]	14	[E]
5	[C]	15	[C]
6	[D]	16	[D]
7	[E]	17	[C]
8	[C]	18	[F]
9	[C]	19	[F]
10	[E]	20	[C]

MCQ Answers

	A	B	C	D	E		A	B	C	D	E
21	T	T	F	F	F	45	T	T	T	F	T
22	T	T	T	T	F	46	T	F	F	T	T
23	T	T	T	T	T	47	F	F	T	T	T
24	T	F	T	T	T	48	F	F	F	T	T
25	T	T	T	T	T	49	T	T	F	T	T
26	F	T	F	F	T	50	T	T	T	F	T
27	F	T	F	T	F	51	T	F	F	F	F
28	T	F	F	F	T	52	T	T	T	T	T
29	F	T	T	T	F	53	F	T	T	T	T
30	T	F	T	T	T	54	F	T	T	F	T
31	T	T	F	T	T	55	T	T	F	F	T
32	F	T	T	F	F	56	F	F	T	F	T
33	T	F	T	T	F	57	T	F	T	F	T
34	F	T	F	T	T	58	T	T	T	F	F
35	T	T	T	T	F	59	T	T	F	T	F
36	T	F	F	T	F	60	F	T	T	F	T
37	T	F	T	F	T	61	T	T	T	T	T
38	F	T	F	F	T	62	F	F	F	T	T
39	F	F	F	T	T	63	F	T	T	T	F
40	T	T	T	F	F	64	T	T	T	F	T
41	F	F	T	T	T	65	T	T	T	F	F
42	F	T	T	F	T	66	T	F	T	F	F
43	T	T	T	T	T	67	T	F	F	F	F
44	F	T	T	F	T	68	T	F	T	T	T